Mini-Moments
for
Graduates

Mini-Moments
for
Graduates

by Robert Strand

New Leaf Press

First printing: February 1996
Fifth printing: February 2005

ISBN: 0-89221-318-3
Library of Congress Number: 95-73128

Printed in the United States of America.

Please visit our website for other great titles:
www.newleafpress.net

For information regarding author interviews, please contact the publicity department at (870) 438-5288.

Presented to:

_____

Presented by:

_____

Date:

_____

The Chinese Bamboo

Too many graduates tend to think only in the short term! And any graduate who doesn't take the long look will eventually be doomed to failure.

Think about the Chinese Bamboo. The bamboo seed is a nut with a very tough skin, so after it's planted it must be watered and fertilized. But the first year nothing happens.

More watering and fertilizing a second year and nothing happens . . . the same process is repeated through the third and fourth years, still nothing. Then in the fifth year the stalk bursts through the ground and in a period of six weeks the Chinese bamboo grows some 90 feet tall!

Did the bamboo grow 90 feet in six weeks or 90 feet in five years? When taking the long look, or for that matter if you only consider the present, remember the bamboo from China! Therefore, do not give up on any seed of future potential!

It takes a great person to give sound advice
tactfully . . . but even a greater person to
accept it graciously and act upon it.

*Trust in the L*ORD *with all your heart*
and lean not on your own
understanding; in all your ways
acknowledge him, and he will make
your paths straight (Prov. 3:5–6).

Read it Through

A young man from a wealthy family was about to graduate from high school. It was the custom in that community for the parents to give the graduate a car. Bill and his father had spent months looking, and the week before graduation they found the perfect car. Bill was positive it would be his!

Imagine his disappointment when, upon graduation, Bill's father handed him a gift-wrapped Bible! He was so angry he threw the Bible down and stormed out. He and his father never saw each other again. It was the news of his father's death that finally brought Bill home again.

As he sat going through his father's possessions, he came across the Bible his father had given him. He brushed away the dust and opened it to find a cashier's check, dated the day of his graduation, for the exact amount of the car!

Thankfulness can well be one of the finest sentiments of humanity and it might also be one of the rarest.

Be joyful always; pray continually; give thanks in all circumstances, for this is God's will for you in Christ Jesus (1 Thess. 5:16–18).

A thorough knowledge of the Bible
is worth more
than a college education.

Theodore Roosevelt (1858–1919)

Goals

Statistics tell me that if I were to poll each of you, less than 5 percent of you could tell me what your life goal is! Ninety-five out of every 100 people seem to be moving with the tides of life and chance.

An eight-year-old boy told his mother and everyone who would listen to him, "I am going to be the greatest baseball catcher that ever lived!" People laughed at him.

His mother told him, "You are eight years old; that's not the time to be talking about impossible dreams." In high school, as he walked across the platform to receive his diploma, the school superintendent stopped him and said, "Johnny, tell us what you want to be."

The young man squared his shoulders and said, "I am going to be the greatest baseball catcher that ever lived!" And you could hear the snickers across the crowd. But history and the record books confirm that Johnny Bench went on to become, according to Casey Stengel, the greatest baseball catcher that ever played the game!

Real leaders are very ordinary people with extraordinary determination.

Cast your bread upon the waters, for after many days you will find it again (Eccles. 11:1).

Covering All the Bases

A little girl was overheard talking to herself as she walked through her backyard, baseball cap in place and carrying softball and bat. "I'm the greatest women's softball player in the world," she said proudly.

Then she tossed the softball in the air, swung, and missed. Undaunted, she picked up the softball, threw it in the air, and said to herself, "I'm the greatest softball player ever!" She swung at the ball again, and again she missed. She paused a moment to look at the bat carefully and the softball carefully.

Then once more she threw the ball into the air and said, "I'm the greatest women's softball player who ever lived." She swung real hard and missed again.

"Wow!" she exclaimed. "What a world-class pitcher!"

And now here is my secret, a very simple secret; it is only with the heart that one can see rightly, what is essential is invisible to the eye. (Antoine de Saint-Exupery)

The Sovereign LORD is my strength; he makes my feet like the feet of a deer, he enables me to go on the heights (Hab. 3:19).

You Are a Marvel

Each second we live is a new and unique moment of the universe, a moment that will never be again. And what do we teach our children? We teach them that two and two make four, and that Paris is the capital of France.

When will we also teach them what they are?

We should say to each of them: "Do you know what you are? You are a marvel. You are unique. In all the years that have passed, there has never been another child like you. Your legs, your arms, your clever fingers, the way you move.

"You may become a Shakespeare, a Michelangelo, a Beethoven. You have the capacity for anything. Yes, you are a marvel. And when you grow up, can you then harm another who is, like you, a marvel?"

(Pablo Casals)

Everybody can be great . . . because anybody can serve. You don't have to have a college degree to serve. You don't have to make your subject and verb agree to serve. You only need a heart full of grace. A soul generated by love. (Martin Luther King Jr.)

When the righteous thrive, the people rejoice; when the wicked rule, the people groan (Prov. 29:2).

*Today one has to pass more tests
to get into college
than Dad had to pass
to get out.*

True Grit

Steve Genter of Lakewood, California, was a participant at the Munich Olympics for the USA. Less than one week before the competition, while in training, one of his lungs collapsed! The doctors made an incision, repaired the lung, put the stitches in, and taped him up. "Well," everybody said, "too bad, this poor kid's out of the competition."

To the consternation of the crowd, when they called his name, he stepped to the starting block as part of the 200 meter freestyle swim event. Going into the 100 meter turn, halfway, in a dead heat with Mark Spitz, he hit the wall to make his turn and tore the stitches loose. This threw his timing off, but he swam on and finished second. Spitz beat him by less than 1/10 of a second. He continued to swim, to compete . . . and Steve went on to win a gold medal, a silver medal I just told you about, and a bronze medal! Success can come out of defeat!

If you have made up your mind you can do something . . . you're absolutely right!

One thing I do: Forgetting what is
behind and straining toward what is
ahead, I press on toward the goal to
win the prize for which God has called
me heavenward in Christ Jesus
(Phil. 3:13–14).

Change It or Live It

Alexander the Great had a man in his army who had the same exact name as the great commander . . . but the man was a coward! Into battle they'd go, but this man would run or find some excuse not to fight. Word leaked back up through the ranks to Alexander and he sent for the man. As the soldier stood before the commander with fear and trembling, Alexander said to him, "You will either change your name or change your conduct!"

That goes for a lot of us. If you name it . . . you'd better live it! When you call yourself a Christian, you must conduct your business, enjoy your leisure, plan your life, treat others, cast your vote . . . all in harmony with your citizenship in heaven.

The life actions we do should reflect exactly who and what we really are. What this world is looking for is not only a Christ to be worshiped but a Christ in blue jeans! A believable lifestyle.

Don't measure yourself by what you
have accomplished, but by what you should
have accomplished with your gifts,
talents, and abilities.

*Now when Daniel learned that the
decree had been published, he went
home to his upstairs room where the
windows opened toward Jerusalem.
Three times a day he got down on his
knees and prayed, giving thanks to his
God, just as he had done before*
(Dan. 6:10).

F. Q.

Did you know that there is a characteristic, a mental attitude, that you can develop which will insure success in life? A group of West Coast psychologists and psychiatrists isolated a single element that they discovered can be found in people who are considered "successful" in their work. It was a common denominator which they called "F.Q." (Failure Quotient).

F.Q. is the ability of a person who fails to come back from that failure. They went on to say that everybody experiences failures in life, but the people who are a success come back, overcome, rise above, or fight it through. In their research with people from all walks of life, they found it was how people coped with failure that was the deciding factor in life.

What does failure do to you? To some of us, it's sort of like a warm pigpen, comfortable to stay in. So we can stay down and rationalize or pick ourselves up and try again! That's what success is all about . . . turning defeat into success!

Accept the challenges so that you may feel
the exhilaration of victory.
(General George S. Patton)

*Do not let this Book of the Law
depart from your mouth; meditate on
it day and night, so that you may be
careful to do everything written in it.
Then you will be prosperous and
successful* (Josh. 1:8).

Everything requires effort:
the only thing you can achieve
without it is failure.

Enthusiasm

This is one life quality that most people are for. But it is also one of the most fascinating and misunderstood qualities of life.

One example of how enthusiasm for a product has skyrocketed the demand is seen in the hen. Yes, you read it right, a chicken. When a hen lays an egg, which is an all-day job in most cases, she cackles and excitedly announces in her proudest fashion that she has produced another. On the other hand, a duck hen lays an egg and is passive about the whole thing. All of us know the demand of chicken eggs over duck eggs is much greater . . . even though a typical duck egg is two to three times larger than a chicken's egg!

The word enthusiasm comes from two Greek words, *en* and *theos*, which literally means "God is within you!" Enthusiasm, *"en-theos!"* And this life quality is catching!

To become enthusiastic is never an accident; it is always the result of high intention, sincere effort, intelligent direction, and skillful execution. It represents the wise life choice.

The LORD your God is with you, he is mighty to save. He will take great delight in you, he will quiet you with his love, he will rejoice over you with singing (Zeph. 3:17).

You Must Go Through Rome

Frank Budd had just finished running the hundred-yard dash in 9.2 seconds in the national championships! It was a new world record! People crowded around him, reporters clamored for a word or two. Reporter Bob Richards said, "Frank, this is a little different than Rome, isn't it?"

Frank Budd sobered as he remembered. Few people knew what Richards had referred to, but Frank knew. In the previous year, Frank had been a part of our Olympic mile relay team. He was the number three man to run in that four-man relay team. When it was the moment for Frank to hand the baton off to Ray Norton, who ran the last leg, Frank fumbled the baton, and in the bobble Norton went out of the exchange area and we lost what would have been four gold medals and a new world record. Then, in the roar of the crowd, Frank sobered and said, "You've got to go through Rome to appreciate a moment like this!"

Failure is God's shock treatment.
(Nels Ferrer)

If we claim to be without sin, we
deceive ourselves and the truth is not
in us. If we confess our sins, he is
faithful and just and will forgive us
our sins and purify us from all
unrighteousness (1 John 1:8–9).

Which Am I?

I watched them tearing a building down
A gang of men in a busy town,
With ho-heave and lusty yell
They swung a beam and a side wall fell;
I asked the foreman, "Are these men skilled
As the men you'd hire to build?"

He gave a laugh and said, "No, indeed!
Just common labor is all I need;
I can easily wreck in a day or two what
Builders have taken a year to do!"
And I thought to myself as I went away
Which of these roles have I tried to play?

Am I a builder who works with care,
Measuring life by rule and square?
Am I shaping my deed to well-made plan,
Patiently doing the best I can?
Or am I a wrecker, who walks this town
Content with the labor of tearing it down?
(Jess Kenner)

**It is quality rather than quantity
that matters.** (Seneca)

*Why then do you tolerate the treacherous? Why
are you silent while the wicked swallow up those
more righteous than themselves?* (Hab. 1:13).

The Touchstone

Legend has it that one day a traveler stopped at a happy farmer's home and talked about life and beautiful foreign lands. He told the farmer about the "touchstone." It could be found on the shores of the Black Sea and anything it touched would turn to gold and the owner would be rich beyond his fondest dreams. The "touchstone" would be identified by the feel, warmer than the other stones. So the farmer sold his farm, placed his family with neighbors, and went in search of the touchstone.

On the shores of the Black Sea he picked up a stone, felt it, found it cool, and dropped it. He knew he must have a plan or he could pick up the same stone many times. So he picked up a stone, felt it, found it cool, then threw it into the sea. Day after day, week after week, year after year it went on. One day he picked up a stone, it was warm to the touch, the TOUCHSTONE . . . and he threw it into the sea. WHY? Habit had been so strong that when he found it, he also threw it away! What's your touchstone? CHOICE! Exercise it well, value it highly!

> We have always held to the hope, the belief, the conviction, that there is a better life, a better world, beyond the horizon.
> (Franklin D. Roosevelt)

But if serving the LORD seems undesirable to you, then choose for yourselves this day whom you will serve, whether the gods your forefathers served beyond the River, or the gods of the Amorites, in whose land you are living. But as for me and my household, we will serve the LORD (Josh. 24:15).

*See some good picture — in nature, if possible,
or on a canvas — hear a page of the best
music, or read a great poem every day. You
will always find a free half hour for one
or the other, and at the end of the year your mind
will shine with such an accumulation of jewels as
will astonish even yourself.*

Henry Wadsworth Longfellow (1807–1882)

Decisive!

This world seems to be divided into three classes of people . . . those who make things happen; those who watch things happen; and those who don't know anything has happened.

There's an anecdote from the dramatic story of General Curtis LeMay. It seems that the general was in an old "flying boxcar" airplane, carelessly puffing on a cigar. A young officer, fresh from training school, angrily approached another officer to complain bitterly, "What's the matter with that old fool? Doesn't he know the aircraft is a firetrap? It could blow up!"

To which the other officer calmly replied, "It wouldn't dare."

In our age of too many weak-willed, wimpy people, it's refreshing to find decisive people! It's the people who can make a decision who also make things happen. This is one ingredient common to that group of people who make things happen. Our world is looking for many more decisive people!

One person with courage makes a majority.

Simply let your "Yes" be "Yes," and
your "No," "No"; anything beyond
this comes from the evil one
(Matt. 5:37).

To Catch a Monkey

One of the oldest methods of catching monkeys is so simple we may doubt that it works. But there's lots of evidence to the contrary. A monkey hunter merely cuts a small hole in a gourd, ties it to a post or tree in monkey territory, then places some seeds in the hollowed-out gourd. Before long, a monkey comes by and is overwhelmed by curiosity, and reaches through the tiny hole to explore the gourd's contents. Feeling the seeds, it scoops them up in a hand and tries to pull this fist through the tiny hole. Trapped! Because the monkey thinks this is some kind of treasure, it will not let go, but keeps the seeds tightly grasped until captors come.

The monkey could free itself simply by letting go. Could some of our own life actions be as foolish as the monkey's? How many of us will hold on to material things so tightly that we will be caught in the frustration of the material? How many hold on to seeds of pleasure, drugs, habits until we are captured?

A "no" uttered from the deepest conviction
is better and greater than a "yes" merely
uttered to please, or what is worse, to avoid
trouble. (Mahatma Gandhi)

*Then he said to them, "Watch out! Be
on your guard against all kinds of
greed; a man's life does not consist in
the abundance of his possessions"*
(Luke 12:15).

Piltdown Man

For more than 40 years the "Piltdown Man" was an honored member of the society of earliest humans. Then a startling discovery proved him to be an enormous fraud. The story has been told in the book *The Piltdown Forgery,* by anthropologist J. S. Weiner.

In early 1912, fossil hunter Charles Dawson brought the first finds of the Piltdown Man to the British Museum. Immediately the finder became famous and soon other fragments of the missing link began coming in from Dawson. The find was named "Eoanthropus dawsoni" or "Dawson's Dawn Man." About 40 years later, scientists found that Dawson had deceived them. The jaw had come from a modern day ape, with the faker "fossilizing" it by staining it mahogany with iron salt and bichromate. Then an oil paint, probably red sienna, had stained the chewing surfaces of the teeth. Further tests revealed that every fragment of the

Piltdown Man was a forgery, a fake! It was one of the greatest hoaxes perpetrated on the scientific community!

A man who has never gone to school may steal from a freight car, but if he has a university education, he may steal the whole railroad. (Theodore Roosevelt)

He who works his land will have abundant food, but the one who chases fantasies will have his fill of poverty (Prov. 28:19).

*The dictionary
is the only place
where success
comes before work.*

Critics and Success

It is not the critic who counts, not the man who points out how the strong man stumbles or where the doer of deeds could have done them better. The credit belongs to the man who is actually in the arena, whose face is marred by dust and sweat and blood.

Who strives valiantly.

Who errs and comes short again and again because there is no effort without error and shortcomings, who knows the great devotion.

Who spends himself in a worthy cause.

Who at best knows in the end the high achievement of triumph and who at worst, if he fails while daring greatly, knows his place shall never be with those timid and cold souls who know neither victory nor defeat!

(Theodore Roosevelt)

Well-done is better than well-said.
(Benjamin Franklin)

And whatever you do, whether in word
or deed, do it all in the name of the
Lord Jesus, giving thanks to God the
Father through him (Col. 3:17).

Risking

To laugh is to risk appearing the fool.

To cry is to risk appearing too sentimental, too weak.

To reach out for another is to risk involvement.

To place your ideas, your dreams before the crowd is to risk their loss.

To love is to risk not being loved in return.

To live is to risk dying.

To hope is to risk despair.

To try is to risk failure.

But risks must be taken because the greatest hazard in life is to risk nothing.

The person who risks nothing, does nothing, has nothing, and is nothing.

ONLY THE PERSON WHO RISKS IS FREE!

God holds us responsible, not for what we
have, but for what we could have . . . not for
what we are, but for what we might be.

Listen . . . accept what I say, and the
years of your life will be many. . . .
Hold on to instruction, do not let it
go; guard it well, for it is your life
(Prov. 4:10–13).

Don't Be Afraid to Fail

You've failed many times, although you may not remember.

You fell down the first time you tried to walk.

You almost drowned the first time you tried to swim, didn't you?

Did you hit the ball the first time you swung a bat?

Heavy hitters, the ones who hit the most home runs, also strike out a lot.

R.H. Macy failed seven times before his store in New York caught on.

English novelist John Creasey got 753 rejection slips before he published 564 books.

Babe Ruth struck out 1,330 times, but he also hit 714 home runs.

Don't worry about failure. Worry about the chances you miss when you don't EVEN TRY![1]

The person who becomes a success in life is
the person who does more than is necessary
to simply get by . . . and keeps on doing it.

*The LORD will make you the head, not
the tail. If you pay attention to the
commands of the LORD your God that
I give you this day and carefully
follow them, you will always be at the
top, never at the bottom*
(Deut. 28:13).

*Three qualities are vital to success:
toil, solitude, and prayer.*

Carl Sandburg (1878–1967)

The Valued Book

A man who was a keen lover of rare books met an unbookish fellow who had just thrown out an old family Bible. It had been packed away for generations in the attic of his ancestral home.

"Somebody named Guten-something-or-other had printed it," he added.

"Not Gutenberg!?" gasped the book lover. "You have just thrown away one of the first books ever printed. One copy recently sold at Christie's at auction for $600,000!"

The other man, still unmoved, said, "Oh, yes, but my copy wouldn't have brought a dime because some guy by the name of Martin Luther had scribbled notes all over it."

Your Bible may not be worth that much, monetarily . . . but in reality, the wisdom for living it contains may well be worth much more to you. It's the "how-to-succeed-in-life" book for all of us!

The study of the Bible is a post-graduate course based on the richest library of human experience.

Do your best to present yourself to God as one approved, a workman who does not need to be ashamed and who correctly handles the word of truth (2 Tim. 2:15).

An Inside Job

In a Southern California university an interesting exhibition was conducted. The scientist took a glass beaker which had a small neck and was enlarged to about seven inches in diameter below the neck. This particular beaker had been specially tempered and treated. The demonstrator used the glass beaker as a hammer to drive a spike into a wooden plank! It was so well-tempered that the fragile-looking beaker did not break! Then . . . he took a small steel ball bearing, about the size of a pea, and dropped it inside the beaker while holding it at the neck. When the ball bearing hit bottom, the glass shattered and the beaker was broken from the blow inside.

This is much like life — it's not the blows from the outside that break us, it's the little things from the inside. In reality, life consists of 10 percent of the things which happen to us on the outside, but about 90 percent from the inside in how we react to what happens to us.

> I was not delivered into this world in defeat, nor does failure course in my veins. I am not a sheep waiting to be prodded by my Shepherd. I am a lion and I refuse to talk, to walk, to sleep with the sheep. (Og Mandino, from the ancient scroll marked "III" in *The Greatest Salesman in the World*)

> *Do not pay attention to every word people say* (Eccles. 7:21).

This Nation

During the difficult days of the Constitutional Convention, when agreement seemed next to impossible, Benjamin Franklin, who had not always been so religious, stressed the necessity of prayer. He was an old man and felt that if the new nation didn't place its trust in God it would fail. We are told that as he came out of the convention hall, a lady asked him, "What shall it be, Mr. Franklin, a monarchy or a republic?"

He replied, "A republic . . . if YOU can keep it!"

Franklin's statement is significant at this point in our history. On July 4, 1776, 56 men signed their names to a unique document which we cherish as our Declaration of Independence. In so doing they willingly laid down their lives to create this nation. Now it is up to the current generation to keep this nation free and growing because the battle is still on to keep it!

Some day, when men don't have to risk
their lives for it, this freedom will
seem an easy thing.

(George Washington at Valley Forge)

*I urge, then, first of all, that requests,
prayers, intercession and thanksgiving
be made for everyone — for kings and
all those in authority, that we may live
peaceful and quiet lives in all
godliness and holiness. This is good,
and pleases God our Savior*
(1 Tim. 2:1–3).

Many learned men,
with all the rich furniture of their brain,
live and die slaves to the spirit
of this world.

William Law (1686–1761)

The Flying Teakettle

A car wreck in 1906 changed the face of the auto industry and may have been largely responsible for much of the air pollution today! The auto industry was in the throes of indecision with two choices: steam propulsion or gas powered. Steam seemed best until. . . .

The annual races were held in Ormond, Florida, in which several cars had unsuccessfully tried to reach 100 mph. Then the "Stanley Steamer," nicknamed the "Flying Teakettle," took the track. Fred Marriott, the driver explains, "I quickly got up to 127 miles per hour and the speed was still rising fast when the car hit a bump. I felt it twist a little in the air, it rose off the beach and traveled about a hundred feet through the air before it struck. I was thrown clear. The machine broke to pieces with the boiler rolling and blowing steam like a meteor for a mile down the beach." John Carlova, auto expert, says this was the turning point when gas became the choice.

Decisions can easily set lifetime directions! Choose wisely!

Choice . . . not chance, is what will
determine destiny.

*The wise heart will know the proper
time and procedure. For there is a
proper time and procedure for every
matter* (Eccles. 8:5–6).

Black Bart

A handkerchief that was dropped brought an end to the career of California's most colorful stagecoach robber. "Black Bart" had terrorized stages for six years, committing 28 robberies between 1877 and 1883 in the rugged foothills of the Sierras. He dressed in a long black linen duster with a flour sack over his head. He would hold his shotgun on the driver and ask, "Will you please throw down your treasure box, sir?"

Finally, near Copperopolis, Bart was wounded while escaping a holdup and dropped a handkerchief with the laundry mark "FXO7." This was traced to San Francisco where police made one of the most surprising arrests in the city's history. "Black Bart," stagecoach robber, turned out to be Charles E. Bolton, one of the city's leading citizens. He had a reputation as a non-smoking, non-drinking, God-fearing man with big business interests in gold mines. He confessed his crimes and was sentenced to six years in San Quentin.

Black Bart wasn't the first nor the last to live a lie. Deception is a poor way to live!

Too many people are thinking that crime is
not crime until a discovery makes it so.

Blessed are those who wash their robes, that they
may have the right to the tree of life and may go
through the gates into the city. Outside are the dogs,
those who practice magic arts, the sexually immoral,
the murderers, the idolaters and everyone who loves
and practices falsehood (Rev. 22:14–15).

Horatio Alger

Horatio Alger wrote over 100 rags-to-riches novels until his name became synonymous with going from poverty to riches. But if he had written his own personal story, he definitely would have given it a different ending. Alger's characters always ended up triumphant, happy, and rich. He earned incredible wages for his day. But he wasn't happy nor comfortable with his success. He simply squandered his money on poker. His books were prized and often given as awards in Sunday school contests. As his books grew more popular, his interests began to wander. He tried to produce a play, then run a curio shop — both failed. He chased fire engines so he could watch the flames. He ended his days writing epitaphs for himself. Among them was this favorite of his: "Here lies a good fellow who spent his life while he had it."

Life is much more than experiencing only financial success!

Success makes failures out of
too many people.

*Naked I came from my mother's
womb, and naked I will depart. The
L*ORD *gave and the L*ORD *has taken
away; may the name of the
L*ORD *be praised*
(Job 1:21).

Periods

Roger van Oech, author of *A Whack on the Side of the Head,* tells this: When I was a sophomore in high school, my English teacher put a small chalk dot on the blackboard. He asked the class what it was. Some time passed, then someone said, "A chalk dot on the blackboard." The rest of the class seemed relieved that the obvious had been stated.

"I'm surprised at you," the teacher told the class. "I did the same exercise yesterday with a group of kindergartners and they thought of 50 different things the chalk mark could be: an owl's eye, cigar butt, the top of a telephone pole, a star, pebble, button, rotten egg, and so on."

In the ten-year period between kindergarten and high school, not only had we learned how to find the right answer, we had also lost the ability to look for more than one right answer. We learned how to be specific, but we had lost much of our imaginative power.

Children enter school as question marks
and leave as periods. (Neil Postman)

*But the one who received the seed that
fell on good soil is the man who hears
the word and understands it.
He produces a crop, yielding a
hundred, sixty or thirty times what
was sown* (Matt. 13:23).

*God will not look you over for
medals, degrees, or diplomas,
but for scars.*

Elbert Green Hubbard (1856–1915)

Absentmindedness

One of this world's greatest scientists was also recognized as the original absent-minded professor. One day on board a train, he was unable to find his ticket. The conductor said, "Take it easy, you'll find it."

When the conductor returned, the professor still couldn't find his ticket. The conductor, recognizing Albert Einstein said, "I'm sure you bought a ticket. Forget about it."

"You're very kind," he said to the conductor, but then with urgency, "but I must find it, otherwise I won't know where to get off!"

Destinations are important! Beginnings are important, too . . . but the end result has a finality about it. As you travel through life think about the ultimate, future destination. Where will your life end? How will you arrive at your final destination? Where and what will it be?

Too many of us are like the person who flung himself on his horse and rode off in all directions at the same time.

There is a time for everything, and a season for every activity under heaven: a time to be born and a time to die (Eccles. 3:1).

Viewpoint

Two ladies were leaning over the guardrail of a 50-story skyscraper . . . the rail broke and both fell. As they passed the 15th floor, the pessimist of the two was heard to say, "Helppp!"

The other, an optimistic lady, yelled, "So far, so gooood!"

Viewpoint, perspective, attitude . . . is the glass half empty or half full? Is it a stoplight or a golight? Is it partly cloudy or partly sunny? It may not change the reality of the situation, but your attitude affects not only me, but all the people around you.

Two salespersons were sent to an emerging country to sell shoes. The pessimistic salesperson faxed back, "Send me a ticket home. Nobody here wears shoes!"

The other, optimistic, faxed, "Nobody wears shoes over here! Everybody is a prospect for our product. Send more shoes, more samples, more order blanks, and some more help!"

Are you looking at obstacles or opportunities, is life half empty or half full for you?

Most people sort of hope for the best . . .
but an optimist actually expects to get it.

Dear friends, build yourselves up in your most holy faith and pray in the Holy Spirit. Keep yourselves in God's love as you wait for the mercy of our Lord Jesus Christ to bring you to eternal life
(Jude 20–21).

What Really Is Success?

That person has achieved success who has lived well, laughed often, and loved much.

Who has gained the respect of intelligent people and the love of little children.

Who has filled a special niche in life, and finished their task.

Who has left the world a better place than they found it,

Whether by developing an improved flower, or writing an uplifting poem,

Or having rescued somebody who might have fallen.

Who has never lacked an appreciation of this earth's beauty or failed to express it,

Who has always looked for the best in others and given their best to others.

Whose life was an inspiration to others; who served God well.

Whose memory is a benediction!

Total success is the continuing involvement
in the pursuit of a worthy ideal, which is
being realized for the benefit of others . . .
rather than at their expense.

(Dennis Waitley)

*Jesus replied: "Love the Lord your God with all your
heart and with all your soul and with all your mind.
This is the first and greatest commandment. And the
second is like it: Love your neighbor as yourself. All
the Law and the Prophets hang on these two
commandments"* (Matt. 22:37–40).

Education is not the filling of a pail,
but the lighting of a fire.

William Butler Yeats (1865–1939)

I'd Rather Watch a Winner

I'd rather watch a winner, than hear one any day,
I'd rather have one walk with me than merely show the way.
The eye's a better pupil and more willing than the ear;
Fine counsel is confusing, but example's always clear.
And the best of all the coaches are the ones who live their creeds;
For to see the good in action is what everybody needs.
I can soon learn how to do it if you'll let me see it done;
I can watch your hands in action, but your tongue too fast may run.
And the lectures you deliver may be very wise and true;
But I'd rather get my lessons by observing what you do.
For I may misunderstand you and the high advice you give;
But there's no misunderstanding how you act and how you live.
I'd rather watch a *winner*, than hear one any day!

Edgar A. Guest poem "Sermons We See"

(I have substituted "winner" in place of "sermon" in the poem and changed the title)

You get out of life what you plant and more . . . plant acorns and you get oak trees; plant seeds of great ideas and you get great people.

Now all has been heard; here is the conclusion of the matter: Fear God and keep his commandments, for this is the whole duty of man (Eccles. 12:13).

Behind the Golden Arches

Ray Kroc, founder of "McDonald's" is the story of one man who had a dream and never gave up on it. He didn't hit his stride until he was 52. His career began by selling paper cups for 17 years. He gave it up and started all over again in the milkshake machine business. Then he heard that the McDonald brothers in San Bernardino were turning out 40 milkshakes at one time on eight of his multi-mixer machines, so he went to check them out. After looking at the operation he asked the brothers, "Why don't you open other restaurants like this?"

They replied, "It would be a lot of trouble," and that they didn't know who they'd get to open them. Ray Kroc had such a person in mind — Ray Kroc.

He bought them out and began a new business at 52. He built McDonald's into a BILLION DOLLAR BUSINESS in 22 years! It took IBM 46 years and Xerox 63 years to achieve this level in sales revenues! The key is perseverance and paying your dues!

> As long as you're green you're growing; as
> soon as you're ripe, you start to rot.
> (Old saying)

> *Blessed is the man who perseveres*
> *under trial, because when he has stood*
> *the test, he will receive the crown of*
> *life that God has promised to those*
> *who love him* (James 1:12).

Words to Forget	*Words to Remember*
I can't	I can
I'll try	I will
I have to	I want to
should have	will do
could have	my goal
if only	next time
yes, but	I understand
problem	opportunity
difficult	challenging
impossible	possible
I, me, my	you, your, yours
hate	love

You can go where you want to go, do what
you want to do, have what you want to
have, and be what you want to be.
(Zig Ziglar)

*Jesus looked at them and said, "With
man this is impossible, but not with
God; all things are possible with God"*
(Mark 10:27).

God wishes each of us to work as hard as we can, holding nothing back but giving ourselves to the utmost, and when we can do no more, that is the moment when the hand of divine protection is stretched out to us and takes over.

Don Orione (1872–1940)

The Big Bang

One of America's major symphony orchestras, and I can't recall what city, which may be for the better, gave a stirring performance of Tchaikovsky's "1812 Overture," complete with 16 real live cannons for effect. At the dramatic moment, a problem occurred in the electrical firing system, and all 16 went off at the same moment! This malfunction triggered the smoke alarms in the building! And maybe more rousing than usual . . . this finale featured fire alarms, fire bells, klaxon horns, and a shower of safety foam from the sprinkler system, all combined with the sirens of six fire engines as the building was being evacuated!

I love exciting endings! How about you? There's something to be said for saving the best for last. Say, graduate, fresh from schooling, how do you plan to end your life? With a bang or a whimper? A glorious home-going or a sizzle in the hot place! It all depends on how you choose to live your life which determines how it will end! I'm for living with eternal values!

> Better never to have been born at all than
> never to have been born again.
> (Eleanor Doan)

*For God so loved the world that he
gave his one and only Son, that
whoever believes in him shall not
perish but have eternal life*
(John 3:16).

King Gillette

Would you like to make your name a household word? Here's how one man did it. William Painter is the man who invented the common bottle cap, and he had a friend, King G. Gillette, who happened to be a traveling salesman. Painter told him he needed to invent something that people could use more than once, but eventually throw away so they would buy more.

In 1895, while exasperated with his dull razor, Gillette had the bright idea that disposable razors would be that perfect invention. Devising a thin steel blade was the problem . . . but 700 blade failures and 51 razor failures later, he got it right in 1903! In about three years he was selling more than 500,000 annually. The rest is history.

Innovation, attention to details, a seed idea, persistence, and a little bit of acquired know-how made it all possible. And there's your formula on how to become a household word!

Inch by inch, anything is a cinch.
(Robert Schuller)

*Blessed is the man who finds wisdom,
the man who gains understanding, for
she is more profitable than silver and
yields better returns than gold. She is
more precious than rubies; nothing
you desire can compare with her*
(Prov. 3:13–15).

Bored

A teenager complained to his father that most of the church hymns were boring . . . too far behind the times, boring tunes, meaningless old words. His father put an end to this conversation, which had been voiced previously, by saying, "If you think you can write better hymns, then why don't you?"

This teen went to his room and began immediately! He wrote his first hymn at age 16! And . . . he continued to write — 349 more! The year was 1690 and if you have been to church lately, most likely you have sung one or more of his songs. Among those he wrote are such standards as "When I Survey the Wondrous Cross" and "Joy to the World."

Feeling bored with this world or the church or life or the music? Then do something about it! Let the world remember you 300 years from now! Oh, yes, that teen's name was Isaac Watts.

Teenagers are people who get a bit too
much of everything . . . including criticism.

*For there is a proper time and
procedure for every matter*
(Eccles. 8:6).

*If a man is called to be a streetsweeper,
he should sweep streets even as Michelangelo
painted, or Beethoven composed music, or
Shakespeare wrote poetry. He should
sweep streets so well that all the hosts of heaven
and earth will pause to say: "Here lived a great
streetsweeper who did his job well."*

Martin Luther King Jr. (1929–1968)

The Mental Burr

William Boice of Phoenix has written the following: "Dear Lord, I have been re-reading the record of the 'rich young ruler' and his obviously wrong choice. But it has set me to thinking. No matter how much wealth he had, he could not . . . ride in a car, have any surgery, turn on a light, buy penicillin, hear a pipe organ, watch TV, wash dishes in running water, type a letter, mow a lawn, fly in an airplane, sleep on an innerspring mattress, or talk on the phone. If he was rich . . . THEN WHAT AM I?"

Now, how is that for a mental burr under your saddle for the rest of today? It confronts all of us with some sort of an inventory check. Just what are and what will be our priorities? Who and what will we serve with our investment of time, talent, and resources? What are the life choices that we will make? Who will we follow? How will we live?

Choice, not chance, will determine your
ultimate, eternal destiny.

*When Jesus heard this, he said to him,
"You still lack one thing. Sell
everything you have and give to the
poor, and you will have treasure in
heaven. Then come, follow me." When
he heard this, he became very sad,
because he was a man of great wealth*
(Luke 18:22–23).

Premature Deaths

When we think of death, we tend to think of old people dying. But death can happen at any time to any of us. Just consider some of these famous people who died young.

ANNE FRANK, the German Jewess who kept that famous diary, died at age 15. THOMAS CHATTERTON, well known English poet, died at 17. KING TUT, probably the most famous of Egyptian pharaohs, died at 18. JOAN OF ARC, the French heroine and remembered as a martyr, died at 19. NATHAN HALE, American hero from the Revolutionary War, died at age 21. JAMES DEAN, the remembered actor, died at 24. GEORGE GIPP, also known as the "Gipper," who was probably the most famous Notre Dame football player, died at 25. NERO, the infamous Roman Emperor who supposedly fiddled while Rome burned, died at age 31.

Death knows no age limits. It can happen to anybody at any time at any age. Which reminds us that any preparation for life after death must be made in advance.

The only thing worse than growing old is to be denied the privilege.

There on the mountain that you have climbed you will die and be gathered to your people, just as your brother Aaron died on Mount Hor and was gathered to his people (Deut. 32:50).

Excellence

"The quality of a person's life is in direct proportion to their commitment to excellence, regardless of their chosen field of endeavor," so said the late Vincent T. Lombardi, one of the best-known football coaches to ever coach. How is excellence attained?

EXCELLENCE can be attained if you . . .

CARE more than others think is wise,
RISK more than others think is safe,
DREAM more than others think is practical,
EXPECT more than others think is possible!

So . . . my graduate friend, why not strive for excellence? Why not live with excellence as one of your goals in life? Anything you might choose to do with your life should be done with excellence!

Excellence is never an accident; it is always
the result of high intention, sincere effort,
intelligent direction, and skillful execution;
it represents the wise choice of many
alternatives. (Willa A. Foster)

*Dear friend, I pray that you may
enjoy good health and that all may go
well with you, even as your soul is
getting along well* (3 John 2).

*Take care of the minutes
and the hours will take care of themselves.*

Lord Chesterfield (1694–1773)

The Goal

Florence Chadwick, the San Diego swimmer, on her first attempt to swim the English Channel stopped just three miles short of the French coast because it was a foggy day and she couldn't see her goal. On her next attempt, the return swim to England, it was a bright and sunny day. She said she made the swim successfully because she could see her goal!

Chris Hagarty, management consultant from Tiburon, California, cites a study made by Yale University of their graduates who had been out of school for 20 years. Three percent of these grads had written down their specific goals; 10 percent had talked in broad terms about what they wanted to do with their lives; 87 percent had not bothered to write it down or even discuss their goals.

The results, according to this study, showed that the 3 percent who had written out their goals had achieved more success, recognition, and money than the other 97 percent combined!

> Living without a goal is like shooting
> without a target. (Benjamin Franklin)

> *I want to know Christ and the power*
> *of his resurrection and the fellowship*
> *of sharing in his sufferings, becoming*
> *like him in his death, and so,*
> *somehow, to attain to the resurrection*
> *from the dead* (Phil. 3:10–11).

Winner Versus Loser

The WINNER is always part of the answer, the loser is always part of the problem.

The WINNER always has a program, the loser always has an excuse.

The WINNER says "Let me do it with you," the loser says, "That's not my job."

The WINNER sees an answer to every problem, the loser sees a problem for every answer.

The WINNER sees a green near every sand trap, the loser sees two or three sand traps near every green.

The WINNER says, "It may be difficult, but it's not impossible," the loser says, "It may be possible, but it's too difficult."

Today's challenge to you is to do all in your power to become that WINNER!

We re-arrange our furniture, our schedules,
our rooms, our figures, and our finances . . .
but how about our attitudes?

*So do not throw away your
confidence; it will be richly rewarded.
You need to persevere so that when
you have done the will of God, you
will receive what he has promised*
(Heb. 10:35–36).

Faithfulness

Gene Stallings tells of an incident when he was the defensive backfield coach of the Dallas Cowboys of the National Football League. Two all-pro players, now retired, Charlie Waters and Cliff Harris, were sitting in front of their lockers after playing a really tough game against their archrivals, the Washington Redskins. It had been a hard-fought game. Both players were still in their uniforms and both sat with heads bowed in utter exhaustion.

Charlie Waters turned to Harris and said, "By the way, Cliff, just what was the final score?"

In our rough and tumble, competitive society, we sometimes fail to remember that excellence isn't always determined by comparing our score to someone else's. Excellence comes from excellent preparation, giving one's best, playing to exhaustion if need be, holding nothing back, no matter what the final score may be.

> Character grows in the soil of experience, with the fertilization of hard work, the watering of desire, and the satisfaction of a job well done.

> *It is not good to have zeal without knowledge, nor to be hasty and miss the way* (Prov. 19:2).

Notes

1 United Technologies Corp., Hartford, CT, from a message published in the *Wall Street Journal* in 1981.